MUDDLED

POEMS BY

RICHARD PORTER

AND

ANDREW D. WHITEHEAD

For Joplin, Missouri.
You deserve better. You deserve worse.

ACKNOWLEDGMENTS

We have a few people we'd like to thank. Aaron Lipe for all of his hard work and the graciousness and patience he displayed in working for our broke asses. Cody White, Julie Ensor, and Kimberly Zerkel for their exceptional advice and criticism. Lisa Brown for her masterful editorial prowess. And, of course, all the bartenders who have encouraged our appetites. Especially those who have had to babysit Rich. We're sure we're forgetting many, and for that we beg your forgiveness. We've already had a few too many.

This Mug Blues

The parts of you withdrawn from me
        may also hide from you,
and, if revealed through one you meet,
        you'll seem a different you.

The Obedient Dog

The obedient dog of Earth has rolled over again
and my meridian finds itself in shadow,
the night nuzzling its soft, black
underbelly into my street.

The other bourgeois homes
glow incandescently, imperviously,
where light bulbs are clicking on
and sitcoms flash on televisions
with handsome faces lowing for flowery praise,
and the bored are getting bored-er,
and their children getting richer,
and somewhere a salmon is being pummeled
to death by a turbine.

I'm the only one out
to see a shooting star fall diagonally
across our stretch of night.
The biggest I've ever seen.
Where will we fit it?

It will fit; a place will be made,
and another epithet accepted;
who else will catch
what the sky will not hold?

Gravity of Objects
for Comet ISON

I bought binoculars to see it better
a little folding set
from the hunting section of a sporting goods store.
I hope the sky clears before dawn.

Back in my car I determine
to pass the time between now and the wee hours
with glasses of beer at the bar.
I test my purchase by looking out across the parking lot.
It's like seeing the future.

I'll drive to the bar,
with disciplined optimism,
splash on some cologne. Then
I'll go out where it's quiet,
where no lights will interfere.
I'll find the white streak in my binoculars.
I'll marvel at its brightness.
I'll relate to its inertia.

Birthday Poem

I belch, and admire my pint of porter
one-quarter gone, belch, and rejoice to know
there are three-quarters more. The rim winks bright,
and the black, it gulps and gulps, and it thirsts
for more. Steeped in the proper vices,
its appetite invites me to indulge.
Light dances round the rim, on the surface
of the black—reflection is rejection,
yet the black engulfs, is a thirsting gulch,
consumes the light and longs for more and more.
I belch, and admire my pint of porter,
take a piss, and decide to have another.

Feb 15, 2008

Thanks for Pulling Over
a drunkard's song for Brandy Poiry

It's no surprise I'm in my cups,
when every moment begs me drink
pint after pint till I throw up.

I lap up porter like a pup,
suck down each round of creamy ink.
It's no surprise I'm in my cups;

I pound my pints till I erupt
and mark the time with hollow clinks,
pint after pint, till I throw up,

then drink some more to fill back up.
I drink myself beyond the brink;
it's no surprise, I'm in my cups.

I close down bars, I dry up pubs,
suck down the evening as it shrinks,
pint after pint, till I throw up.

I pound my pints till I erupt.
I drink myself well past the brink
(it's no surprise I'm in my cups),
pint after pint, till I throw up.

I Think I Left My Liver in Your Couch
for Daniel Valentine and Lanna Jones

I've woken up in stranger places,
awkwardly crammed into tight spaces,
inside a trunk, beneath a sink,
a locker at the roller rink,
a cabinet housing priceless vases.
I've woken up in stranger places.

I've woken up in stranger places,
and to a few less friendly faces.
An ex. A cop. A squirrel. All pissed.
But, I confess, I do not miss
the dignity good drink erases.
I've woken up in stranger places.

Their Truths

They converge Sunday mornings
on the pointy building at the corner.
They confess their sins, profess their truths,
shake hands at the door like street mongers
dealing in the currency of fear.

I sleep late Sundays.
I watch from my porch as they pass in minivans
and SUVs with decals in the back windows,
stick-figure families and their dogs; Gilgamesh and Amon.

They are the freest of the free
in the greatest country in the world
A warming world, it once was flat, now round
and in its youthful prime.

There was time, a certain story tells,
when pigs built homes of wood and brick
and the scariest thing in a certain wolf's mouth
was not his teeth.

Hungover During the Morning Service

for Matthew Kimbrough

I am a man of faith in empty bottles,
rinsed in the sink to be recycled later,
and stored in the pantry until that day.
A man of faith, with faith in emptied bottles,
who gave of themselves to rinse out my gullet,
who patiently await collection day
and long for the burnings of their reformings,
to be reordered, refashioned, and washed,
and filled, once more, in my unending thirst.

No High-Fiving

My eyes are too tired to read
and anyway Sylvia's relentless loathing
was giving me a headache, so now
back in the car outside the library,
with the radio turned off
after finding my emergency supply of Advil empty,
through sunglasses I watch as
some boys apply Bernoulli's principle
with a radio-controlled airplane.
It buzzes like a hedge trimmer,
then lifts and banks
and settles back to earth.
They seem to be having fun,
but there is no high-fiving, no joyous shouts.
Sending the little plane soaring
above the empty, yellow-ribbed parking lot
does not apparently bring exhilaration,
but jealousy. I know the feeling, boys,
all too well. I left my little plane
on the shelf in the library,
and picked up this pen.

Many Favorites

I have many favorites,
mint juleps for instance,
a certain baseball team from St. Louis,
and Sunday morning walks with my dog.

I have a favorite ink pen.
The ball point retracts with a twist.
It knows the switchback
paths of my signature like a Sherpa.
It feels at home in my hand.

But it wasn't my hand that chose the pen,
I fell for its look—
the elegant lines of its barrel, mostly thin,
but thick in the right places,
and the fine blue trail in its wake
like a row of pining suitors.
My grip grew to love what my eye found fetching—
and it makes me wonder
why freckles?
Why dark hair, light eyes?
Why husky voices?

I have other favorites.
I have a favorite doughnut,
in truth I have had many,
always a maple bar
from the little shop on Main.
Each one a new lover.

MUDDLED

Some are gone quickly;
hurried through to get to the next.
Some are savored; knowing
I'll long for it when I'm finished

You Know

for Kimberly Zerkel

Of course I'm in love, I'm always in love.
Which isn't to slight her beauty, her verve,
the various ways she tickles my nerves,
her sensuous voice that's just a touch rough,
but I'd be an ass to set her above
the others who've caught my eye with their curves.
Nevertheless, there's this wink to her swerve
that just drives me wild, I'm sure you'd approve.

Alas, like the rest, she's taken, of course;
shacked up with her beau, a law office clerk,
bit of a jerk, but a jerk with a job.
Which is fine, you know, she's still a resource,
a valuable muse for my current work:
an unending string of heartbroken sobs.

I Regret

Do I regret
leaving her there,
long legs, smooth and
bare to the thigh
in cutoff jeans,
gold in the porch light,
as she leaned against the door frame
and I drove away
from what could have been fun,
dangerous perhaps,
if her husband found out,
but fun, and maybe messy,
with sticky, saccharine emotions
and a foreboding future
of covert meetings and little lies
that roll into one another
like snowflakes on a hill,
that with momentum,
and fateful time,
become a tremendous
crushing mass?
I haven't decided.

Here's the Rub

Tired of touching and tired of being touched,
she stiffens, sighs, and recoils from his touch.
Grown bored with her love, he doesn't mind much.

A shower will do. He'll wash off his urge.
Repetitive force will work out his urge.
No partner's required; it's simply a purge.

Repetitive action. Rinse and repeat.
This time tomorrow, they'll rinse and repeat.
He'll chance an advance. She'll wince and retreat

to lie on the couch and think about rain.
She'll lie to herself. She'll think about rain,
while he rubs one out and stares at the drain.

Grown bored with her love, he doesn't mind much
when she stiffens, sighs, recoils from his touch.

Arm-bar, Duckunder, Headlock

My muse is not a giver,
she must be taken by surprise, tricked,
subdued.
She doesn't give in easily.
It can take several rounds of drinks,
several rounds of hair pulling, arm biting.

My muse is a stubborn,
capricious mistress,
a scornful lover.
She's a taker.
She gets hers first,
I finish in the shower.

My muse is Jacob's angel.
She leaves me hobbled.
I've never known her name.

Keep your rain on the window,
your park bench,
your murky cup of coffee.
Keep your tidy,
gentle muse.
I'll practice my Arm-bar,
Duckunder, Headlock—
We will struggle until sunrise.
She will bless me.
I will face the sun alone.

On Our DNA

Spring had come, and with the wind and tulips
weddings came as well.
Spring is a good time of year
for weddings, I suppose,
in the same way that February is good
for sweethearts and breakfast for oatmeal.
I cinched the pastel colored tie
snugly against the collar of my white shirt
and asked myself where it is written,
except on our DNA,
that we should now be enemies?

As if loving the same woman
should have done anything
but further reconcile our personalities.
But I am not interested now
and neither is he.

In the car upon arriving, I pop a breath mint
and dab on cologne
likes it's the blood of my enemies.
I wear my smile like war paint, we shake hands
like boxers bumping gloves,
I weave with my small-talk questions,
and wield my inquisitive, knotted brow
like a brisk right jab.

I Don't Know What 'Epistemology' Means

for Alice Ensor

It makes life interesting, if tiresome, too,
our charmingly endless gift for misprision,
where hammers see nails in fingers and screws.

Values are warped, in exchanges, through friction.
You rub off the face, you leave bits of you.
And then there are gaps and omissions, elisions.

So, even when right, one's view's slightly skewed
by facts fallen through and info tacked on.
It's true: I can't know you as you know you

and I don't think I'd like to. I've grown fond
of my misreadings, my errant essays.
Getting it wrong is an awkward jouissance.

This is strange, I know, but such is my taste:
To stab in the dark. Then blush. Then erase.

Trading Places

Every summer it happens.
The late sunsets depreciate
to light for the cookouts
and the relative volume
of bike sounds in the street
and locusts in trees
seems to lessen like the novelty
of pink in the clouds.

Tonight the streets have stayed busy
with carloads of people clinging
to the last of the summer's
slow-setting suns.
The cars
and the crickets
compete for my ear.
But my ear,
after a season of porch sitting,
has adapted to listening
through the lily pad sounds

so that what I hear
is the slow decrescendo of song
suspended between
solstice and equinox
and the quiet commotion
of constellations
trading places
in the sky.

MUDDLED

Trees change their clothes,
when no one is looking,
days contract, footballs fly,
and the cars
shuffle past to observe, sightseers
escaping the change of the season,
sparing little time
to observe what is passing.

I Don't Need No Memento Mori

My thought's flesh is of Jacob's shrunken hip,
bone grinding bone to the tune of extinction.
Through each ideation, it gnaws, it rips,
through every reflection, every distinction.

And what seems to lift, what seems affirmation,
small comforts, quaint loves, all smack of evasion.
In every reflection, every distinction,
bone grinds on bone to the tune of extinction.

I Love You, Whathaveyou

It is a problem, perforce, of resilience
and motion, of maintaining composures
both withy and stern, to weather the vectors
of tugs, pulls, and tethers, bevies of springs
bubbling up from within, swept into currents
one would rather not sense; meanwhile, there's this:
"I'll love you forever, even when dead."
One among many attempts at cohesion,
gestures and tokens to stave off commotion,
but nothing stops moving, nothing resists.
Shows of affection, sincere though they be,
are things among things, like barges and bricks.
All objects, all actions, concepts and passions
emerge into streams converging on oceans,
arise and depart in eddies and drifts.
No wonder we pray, no wonder we kiss,
build churches and bars, get married, have kids.

Remember the Words

Wrought-iron chairs encircle wrought-iron tables
shaded from moonlight by brightly colored umbrellas
adorned with various beer-brand insignias.

With a cigarette glowing
between a string and the mirrored A's on the guitar
headstock,
the musical act cracks jokes about drugs and oil spills
between songs, drags, and swigs of beer.
He's been partying for too many years
and his voice doesn't act like it did when the songs were
written.

I wonder, as he plays, and looks blankly across
the crowd that seems to be pleasuring much more in
debauchery
than music, if he's struggling
to recall the exhilaration he once found in performing
or just to remember the words.

Your Lips Say "Last Call," But Your Eyes Say "Last Call."

for Jason Martin

Lost in the shuffle of cocktails and pints,
persists the desire to find a like mind,
a compassionate heart inclined to love
one's virtues, one's foibles, all the above,
but what we call closeness is ill-conceived.
I cannot know you. You cannot know me.
The self is just skin, a surface event,
beneath which becoming churns and ferments.
We're thoroughly muddled, endlessly stirred,
and, drink after drink, we're further unfurled.
I cannot know you. You cannot know me.
What passes as closeness is ill-conceived.
There is only the bar, only the drink,
only the chime of this final shot's clink.